How to Come Out

A Guide for Women
Questioning their Sexual Orientation

Essie Reis

SPIKED Ideas
PUBLICATIONS

Legal Notices

Some of the contributor's names have been change to respect their privacy.

DEDICATION

To the University of Toronto Women's
Coming out Support Group

Table of Contents

Acknowledgement

I would like to thank Chris Alderson for her support and encouragement in the development and editing of this guide.

Introduction

Throughout history lesbians, bisexuals and gays have been kept silent, unnoticed and unseen in an unnecessarily shameful position. It is for this exact reason that today's Pride events are so important in showing that we are not afraid to live 'out and proud' lives.

The progress that LGBT *(Lesbian, Gay, Bisexual and Transgendered)* rights have taken in the last 10 years is phenomenal. It is important however, to give thanks to those who fought for LGBT rights in the past and endured great prejudice, because they have paved the way for us today. While we still have a long way to go, we are on the right path and will pass the torch to the next generation to lead us on to a more giving, loving and prejudice free life in the future.

The LGBT community worldwide is living, loving, marrying, having children and creating families. So, take charge of your life and make it the best you can!

Chris Alderson
Author
Lesbian Film Guide

My Coming Out Story

I came out when I was 23 years old, although I really came out to myself when I was 15. I was raised in a Catholic home where I didn't feel free to be myself. I suffered from depression throughout my teenage years because I felt closeted. I dated men initially, but at 23, after a struggle with thyroid cancer, I realized that life was too short, so I decided to radically change it. I broke up with my boyfriend of 3 years, left home and came out as a lesbian.

While attending the University of Toronto, I joined a coming out group which I later facilitated for several years. This was an extremely important social network that allowed me to freely express myself among women who could relate and understand me. During that time, I came out to my parents, my brother, sister and to my friends. Through this group, I met my first girlfriend and developed solid long term friendships. I developed a sense of pride and confidence that now defines my personality.

Why I Wrote This Book

I wrote this book because my coming out process has been a continuous adventure of challenges, tears and rewards. My intention is to facilitate your coming out process, and serve as a friendly reminder that coming out does not have to be a difficult or painful process, but rather a liberating one which can bring you joy and greater freedom. In this guide, I provide you with direction by giving you recommendations and concrete steps on how to come out to: yourself, your parents, children, and other important people in your life. In addition, I share with you some of my coming out experiences based on diaries I've kept throughout the years. I also share some of the stories of my friends, which they've kindly allowed me to print. I sincerely thank them for their contributions.

Essie Reis

About Sexual Orientation

Sexual orientation refers to feelings of attraction, sexual desires or emotional connections to someone of the opposite sex to your own sex or to both. Sexual orientation also refers to a person's sense of self, identity and how they relate and socialize with others. Research has revealed that one's sexual orientation is not static but moves along a continuum. At its polar ends there is heterosexuality and homosexuality; most people fall somewhere in between. The general labels associated with sexual orientation are: heterosexual: attraction to the opposite sex; homosexual: attraction to the same sex; bisexual: attraction to either sex.

Sexual orientation is more than a biological urge and should not be defined as such exclusively; it encompasses a range of behaviours and actions that reflect one's needs for intimacy and attachment. Since one's sexual orientation usually determines the social activities one engages in, it is usually through those connections that romantic interests are found.

How do you know if you are lesbian or bisexual?

According to studies reported by the American Psychological Association, one's sexual orientation emerges between childhood and early adolescence. If you have had feelings and attraction towards someone of the same sex at any point in your life, you may be lesbian or bisexual, even if you have not had any past sexual experience.

Different people have different experiences regarding their sexual orientation; some women just know they feel an attraction, or a profound connection towards another woman, while they seldom if ever feel that towards a man.

Labelling

The application of a lesbian or bisexual label may vary. Some women need to experience sexual activity with another woman before they feel they can call themselves lesbian. Others will identify as a lesbian without any previous lesbian sexual involvements. Some will only apply that label later on in life once they've had a solid same sex relationship. Many women find it easier to accept a bisexual label, especially if they've had relationships with men and are not certain of the direction they should take. Others will keep the bisexual label, as they feel it truly represents them and does not exclude them from future relationships with men.

What is The Nature of Same Sex Relationships?

Research indicates that many lesbians and bisexual women desire to be in committed long-term relationships. A comprehensive survey conducted in the US revealed that between 40% and 60% of gay men and between 45% and 80% of lesbians are currently involved in long term romantic relationships[1].

---

[1] *American Psychological Association. (2008).*

Why Come Out?

Heterosexuals don't have to worry about coming out as it is assumed in society that they date, love and marry people of the opposite sex. Homosexuals however, don't have this privilege; through their silence they are assumed heterosexual and thus are expected to behave according to the current societal norms that exist in North America.

Research has confirmed that being 'closeted' poses serious psychological risks, including more troubled romantic relationships, distress and even increased suicidal tendencies[2]. Feelings of isolation can ensue, causing social isolation and feelings of alienation. By contrast, research studies indicate that coming out is a good thing. Being open allows lesbians and gays to develop an

---

[2] Published June 2011 in *Social Psychology and Personality Science.*

authentic sense of self and to cultivate a positive self-image.

Stages of Coming Out

What does coming out mean? For many women, it simply means accepting who they are without preconceptions or judgment, assuming an identity that is open and honest, both to themselves and to others around them. To others, it simply means accepting who they are in silence, only sharing their true sexual orientation with a few close friends. Whatever it means to you, what is important is that you accept who you are, that you are comfortable within your own skin, and are not haunted by fears of being discovered and rejected by others. If you carry feelings of a deep dark secret, you are probably not living a carefree and harmonious life. Coming out to yourself in whatever manner you choose, will liberate you from a self-imposed prison and will lead you to living a free and more enjoyable life.

The Cass Theory, developed by Vivan Cass, indicates that people go through a range of stages before coming out and can remain in any one of these stages for an indefinite amount of time.

- Stage One - Identity Confusion: You begin to wonder whether you may be homosexual. Along with other thoughts and feelings, you may experience denial and confusion.

- Stage 2 - Identity Comparison: You accept the possibility that you may be a lesbian and face the social isolation that can occur with this new realization.

- Stage 3 - Identity Tolerance: Your acceptance of your homosexuality increases, and you begin to tolerate yourself better. Although confusion and distress concerning your sexual orientation decreases, you may feel increased isolation and alienation as your self-awareness and self-perception becomes increasingly different from society's and your family's expectation of you. In this stage, you often begin to make contact with members of the LGBT community.

- Stage 4 - Identity Acceptance: You have resolved most of the questions concerning your sexual identity and have accepted yourself as a lesbian. You begin to have increased contact with the LGBT community.

- Stage 5 - Identity Pride: You begin to feel proud of being part of the LGBT community and immerse yourself into LGBT culture. In turn, you have less contact with the heterosexual community and may at times feel anger towards heterosexuals.

- Stage 6 - Identity Synthesis: You integrate your sexual orientation with other aspects of yourself so that it is just one part of your whole identity. The anger you may have felt towards the heterosexual community or the intense pride you may have felt in being homosexual decreases and you can be yourself with both communities. You feel more connected with your public self and your private self. In this final stage, you begin to feel proud of your identity, do not want to hide it and want to share it with people you love, trust and respect. At this point you may experience feelings of pride and truly feel you have come out.

Coming Out To Yourself as a Lesbian or Bisexual

The nature versus nurture argument has been used to explain whether or not homosexuality is genetically based or not. The same research could easily be used to justify a heterosexual orientation. Does it really matter why you are who you are, genetically speaking; lesbian, bisexual or straight? The challenge is to decide how you want to live your life, accepting whatever orientation seems natural and true to you. You can't change who you are, but you can change your perception of yourself and through your behaviour, affect the way others see and relate to you. It all comes down to attitude and self-confidence, although your confidence will definitely improve as you assume your true sexual nature.

If you're reading this, it may mean you're aware that you are not heterosexual and therefore, you're already at stage two or three of the coming out process. You may now just need a few ideas or tips on how to come out in a safe and comfortable way.

Here are some ideas to help you in the process of self-disclosure and full self-acceptance:

1. Research the following online or at your local library:

   - History of homosexuality
   - Your country's (state or province) political position on homosexuality
   - Laws that protect homosexuals in your country, state or province

2. Attend a LGBT event, local, national or international. For example: Pride Day.

3. Read a romance novel involving a lesbian or bisexual character.

4. Watch a movie or TV show with a lesbian or bisexual theme.

5. Start a journal

- Monitor your day and night dreams in your journal. Are they with women? Are you in a female or male role? Try to answer these questions in your journal.

- Do you feel emotionally or sexually drawn to a woman in your life? Write what you are feeling; your journal is your safe space.

- Express your relationship goals. Do you desire intimacy with a woman or man? Do you want to kiss, hug or make love to a woman? Do you feel happy or aroused at the thought of this kind of intimacy? Or do these ideas make you feel uncomfortable or anxious?

- Don't share your journal with anyone; these are your private thoughts and you need to feel free expressing them without anyone judging you.

Finding Support

If you are feeling uncomfortable and have conflicting feelings, you should seek support. Seek a lesbian or gay friendly therapist. You can usually find one at your local LGBT community centre; call ahead to find out if they have lesbian peer counselors. They may also be running coming out groups, which will allow you to connect with others like yourself and instantly meet new people.

If you intend to seek support counselling services online, remember to always do a background check to determine how open minded the therapist is going to be. Read the site's "About Us" page, and seek out information on their philosophy on providing care. A positive therapist will be one that will accept and support you and facilitate your coming out process.

In addition, you can call an LGBT Hotline to talk to someone anonymously. Phone numbers are found in your local phone directly or online *(see resources at the end of this book)*.

Further supports exist online such as through discussion forums and blogs. Forums are great tools that allow you to share your feelings in an anonymous way, while also permitting you to learn from the experience of others. Join the discussions. You'll be amazed at how supported you'll feel.

Blogs are also great tools. See what other women who identify as lesbian or bisexual are talking about. Contribute your opinions to their posts through the "comments" area. Enter key words into the Google search such as: "lesbian blogs" (include the quotes).

Building Self Confidence

Begin to build your self-confidence by practicing the following in front of a mirror:

- I am a gay woman.
- I am a bisexual woman.
- I am a lesbian.
- I love myself.
- I love the fact that I love women.
- I feel attracted to women.
- I desire women sexually.
- I want a relationship with a woman.
- I am proud of who I am.
- I am normal.

If it's difficult to say these words, continue repeating them at least 10-20 times per day. Develop a routine; do it in the bathroom in the morning in front of a mirror or just before going to bed.

Build Self Confidence		
My Affirmations	My Desires	How I'll Overcome My Fears

*Fill out one of these per day and re-read it often.

Once the decision has been made to come out, surround yourself with positive influences. Go to blogs or websites that are affirming; join a social media group such as Facebook; it's a great way to meet new people. Most importantly, have fun! Coming out can be a very exciting time in your life.

How I Came Out to Myself

Coming from a religious background, I was taught that homosexuality was a great sin. I suffered in my youth because I had no one to talk to and knew no other lesbians. I felt so alone and depressed. Sometimes, I even thought about suicide. One day I went to the local library and found a book about lesbians. It didn't judge people rather, it treated them normally. Then I found the book, Desert of the Heart, which depicted a love story between two women. I loved it. I devoured that book, and I read it over and over. Knowing I wasn't alone was so freeing. One day, I flipped through the yellow pages and found a gay/lesbian hotline. I must have called about ten times on many different days, before I had the courage to speak to a live person. I remember my heart pounding as I dialed. I was going to talk to a real lesbian; the thought excited me as much as it frightened me, but one day I did it, I said "hello". Through that phone call, I learned about a coming out group at a local community centre and after months of thinking about it, I dropped by. That was it, I 'came out' and made new friends and began my new life as a lesbian.

Coming Out To Your Friends

Coming out to others is a very personal decision and one that should be made after careful deliberation. Some women simply don't feel the need to come out to anyone, especially their friends for fear of being judged or ridiculed. Others however, feel it is important to let people they care about know that they are not heterosexual and that they should not be treated as such. These women have the need to be truthful and not keep any secrets from the people they most value, often their friends. Coming out to your friends can be a bonding as well as a trust building experience.

Chris's Story

I came out to my cousin Carrie when I was 16 years old. I knew that I was gay and as she was my best friend, I needed to be honest with her. One day I said, "You know, I think I'm gay." She responded with, "yeah, but you like guys too, right?" I felt compelled to say "Yea....Sure," because I was caught off guard. It bothered me that I had not been truthful, so the following day I told her, "You know, I really only like women." She responded "Yeah, I know." From then on, even though we had only discussed it briefly, I knew I could totally be myself with her. I actually watched the first movie with any lesbian content, The Hunger, with her. She asked me during the love scene between Catherine Deneuve and Susan Sarandon, "Is that what you really want to do, kiss another woman?" and I said, "Yes, that's exactly what I want to do."

Are these thoughts holding you back from coming out to your friends?

- Will they stop being my friend?
- Will they stop talking to me?
- Will they tell everyone they know?
- Will they embarrass me?
- Will they 'out' me at work?
- Will they tell my family?

Fear can keep you from getting the support you need. Take the first step;

choose a close friend, someone you trust to confide in. As time goes by, you may decide to come out to your other friends.

The following steps will help you come out to your friends:

Visualize

Thinking about all the possible scenarios and outcomes can be stressful and create a lot of anxiety. Begin to change your way of thinking from the negative to the positive. Go to a room where you will not be disturbed, close your eyes, relax and visualize. Form images in your mind about how you will come out to your friend and visualize him or her having a positive response to you. Do this often and until you feel comfortable and at ease with the notion of being out to your friend.

Engage Conversation

Engage your friend in a discussion about a lesbian issue, for example: What do you think of Pride? How do you feel about lesbian marriages? Listen to your friend, accept whatever opinion he or she expresses to you and then add your opinion, making sure you express a favorable viewpoint. Do not talk over your friend but change conversation if it starts getting heated. If your friend shows acceptance in relation to the lesbian themes of your discussion, you know that he or she may accept you as well.

Watch a Movie

Today, there are many movies or TV shows that have lesbian or bisexual themes. Ask your friend to see one with you. Later, over a coffee or tea, talk about the movie and specifically the lesbian or bisexual character. Make sure you do not judge your friend and always present a positive view of the film and its lesbian or bisexual content (*see the resources included with this package for film ideas*).

Once you start getting positive responses from your friend, you can initiate a discussion about someone you know that is gay or lesbian and how they're living their lives as openly gay people.

Coming Out

When you make the decision to come out as a lesbian or bisexual to your friend, don't plan the day or the time as this may create anxiety for you. However, make up your mind that you will be coming out to your friend when the opportunity presents itself. Make sure you're doing something fun and that you're both in a good mood. The words you use to come out are entirely up to you, some like to say: "I'm a lesbian," "I now identify as lesbian", "I'm attracted to women", " I prefer to only date women" "I am a gay woman", "I am bisexual" and so forth.

Whatever manner you choose, do it with confidence and with the certainty that you'll be accepted. Most likely your friend will feel your positive energy and will accept you wholeheartedly. However, be prepared for all types of reactions as your friend may need time to reflect and adjust to what you have shared. Give your friend the time he or she needs. If they cannot accept you try coming out to another friend.

Research has shown that most people accept their lesbian, gay or bisexual friends with respect and love, although some take longer than others to reach full acceptance[3].

---

[3] Research by a UC Davis Social Psychologist, Herek, G.M. (1997). Heterosexuals' attitudes toward lesbians and gay men: Does coming out make a difference?

How I Came Out to My Friend

When I came out to Angie, my long-time friend from high school, I didn't know what to expect, but I knew I had to tell someone or I was going to explode. We hung around all the time; we talked about everything, so it was only natural to tell her. One day I just said, "I think I'm a lesbian, I hope you're ok with it?" She didn't say much only that she had to go and do something. I felt so hurt. A few days later we met at school and she said she had spoken to her priest. He said to her that we are all God's children and we all deserve love and tolerance. I was touched by the effort, but then she said she could only accept me if I didn't practice my lesbianism. What did that mean? I felt totally betrayed again; after all, I didn't tell her what to do in her personal life, so why should she tell me?

Eventually we grew apart and lost contact. Later on, I took a chance with another long-time friend, who was also religious. She accepted me wonderfully and said that it didn't make any difference if I was lesbian, bi or straight. What mattered was our friendship.

We are still friends to this day.

Coming Out to Your Teenager

Some women may have led heterosexual lives, even marrying and having children prior to coming out. If this is your situation, you may have concerns about how your teenaged son or daughter will accept you and your new found identity. Teenagers are going through their own sexual awakening and the last thing they want to face is their Mom's coming out issues. Nevertheless, it should be dealt with, as secrets will prevent you and your teenagers from properly bonding at a time when they need you the most. Many lesbian parents spend huge amounts of time worrying about how to come out to their teenagers.

Do these questions keep reoccurring in your mind?

- Will they reject me?
- Will they shut down?
- Will they hate me?

- Will they be angry with me?
- Will they run away?

Thinking about all the possible negative scenarios and outcomes can lead to stress and anxiety. Begin to change your way of thinking from 'what will they think of me', to 'how am I going to tell them so they'll accept me with love'.

These phases will help you broach the subject with your teenagers:

Phase 1 – Desensitize I

Bring home books or magazines on lesbian topics and leave them around the house, such as on the coffee table or by the telephone. When your teenager comments on them, just say you find the topic interesting. Do not engage in too much discussion at this time.

Phase 2 – Desensitize II

Rent a movie in which one of the characters is a lesbian or a bisexual woman. Have your teenagers sit down on movie night and watch it with you. At the end, ask what they thought of the movie and especially the lesbian characters. Accept whatever response is given. Do not become defensive in any way, but add your own positive opinion. For example, "I liked the lesbian character, what a great actress".

Phase 3 - Desensitize III

Bring your girlfriend or partner (if you have one) home for a couple of hours. Introduce her to your family only by first name; enjoy a snack or dessert together. If you do not have a girlfriend or partner, engage your teen in a conversation about Ellen DeGeneres or any other 'out' female celebrity. Say that you think they are very brave for having come out and being honest with the world. Then ask how they feel about the subject.

Phase 4 – Discussion

When the opportunity arises and your teenagers mention something about a lesbian or gay friend or schoolmate, seize the moment! Take this opportunity to ask them how they feel about it and encourage discussion on the issue of lesbianism. If their attitude is negative, don't be alarmed or defensive. Just add your own positive viewpoint.

Phase 5 – Come Out

If you have more than one teenager, you may want to come out to one at a time. In this way, you have their undivided attention, and they will not be influenced by the other's reactions.

Choose a day your teen is home alone, approach him or her and ask if you can share something very important and personal. State that you have been hesitant to share it but now feel he or she is mature enough to handle it.

What to say:

- I have come to realize that I am a lesbian.
- I'm attracted to women.
- I now identify as a gay woman.
- I now plan to date women.
- I am bisexual.
- I am in a relationship with a woman.

Wait for their reaction. They may surprise you by hugging you and saying they knew it all along. Whatever the reaction, take it in a positive way. If they become upset, let them express their anger. If they ask you to leave the room, comply and let them take the initiative to return to you later. If they don't return to you, wait a few days and then broach the issue with them. By then, they'll have had time to think about it and to adjust to the notion of Mom as a lesbian.

Questions are a good sign that indicate your teen is making an effort to understand and accept you. Through questions, you'll have the opportunity to share your coming out process. Encourage them to ask you questions, if they don't ask any, lead the conversation by asking your own questions, such as: "You may be wondering when I realized I was a lesbian?" or "You may be wondering why I married your father?"

Don't be surprised if it takes a few days (possibly weeks) for your teenager to accept you and your lesbian identity. Beginning to take steps now will create a more meaningful and stronger relationship between you and your son or daughter.

Phase 6 – Get Support

Seek support from your local LGBT community center and PFlag groups. Begin to pick up brochures, books and films to help you in the coming out process. Most importantly, don't stand alone; ensure you have a good friend, possibly your partner to stand by you for moral support. Keep a positive outlook and that energy will most likely be reciprocated by your teen.

Betty's Story

I came out to my two teens, one at a time, after I had been divorced for over two years. First I told my daughter Lisa, "You know, I haven't been myself lately, maybe you've noticed. It's because I think I'm a lesbian. I think I've always known, but now I think I'm in love with someone at work and it's a woman." Lisa just stared at me, I didn't know if she was going to scream or run off. Then she surprised me by hugging me and saying, "Mom, I'm not surprised, I suspected it; you can't stop talking about that woman at your work. I love you Mom, no matter what."

When I told my son Josh, it was a different story; he just shut down and didn't want to talk about it. A few weeks later he said he was fine with it, and added that he too was gay.

That took me by surprise, but I was glad I was truthful with him, so he too could be honest with me. I often think what if I hadn't come out to him, would he have come out to me? I don't know the answer, but I'm glad I told him. Today, I have no regrets and can honestly say I have gained respect from my children.

Coming Out to Your Children

Young children are very intuitive and often are aware of what's really going on. Most children learn about what is 'normal' and 'not normal' when they begin to interact with others in daycare or school. When they start watching television, they become exposed to many mixed messages about lesbianism and homosexuality. Outside the home, your children may hear conflicting viewpoints on what a typical family looks like. They start comparing themselves with others and seeing other types of families that do not resemble theirs.

Take advantage of the early years when all their time is spent at home with you and your family, do this before their minds are clouded with judgment. Talk openly and sincerely about who you are and how normal your family is. Young children don't need special definitions or special talks; they learn by example and through role modelling. Whatever attitude you have towards lesbians, bisexuals and gays will be the values you instill in your children.

Ensure you are comfortable with yourself, with your relationships, and do not display signs of internalized homophobia. The more positive and natural you are about yourself, the more accepting your children are going to be.

Here are suggested steps to coming out to your young children:

- Talk about lesbian, gay or bisexual topics in a natural way at dinner time.

- Read children's books that address lesbian families and alternative parenting, for example: Heather Has Two Mommies.

- Take your child with you to lesbian friendly events, such as Pride.

- Go to your local LGBT community centre and join PFlag or other parent groups; They often hold fun family events like pot-lucks and BBQ's.

By bringing fun and joyful experiences which involve lesbians, bisexuals and gays into your child's life, you are in fact providing healthy, proud role models. This is the best way to foster within your child a healthy attitude towards LGBT people. These early childhood experiences will most likely act as a shield to outside prejudices and discrimination that may arise later on. Because your children will be raised in a positive, fun filled household, they will be prepared to deal with homophobia on the playground and will likely resist pressures to become homophobic themselves. After all, the most significant influences for your children will come from the people they trust.

As your children grow older, you'll have to reinforce the naturalness of being a lesbian or bisexual, using more mature language, and placing it into a social, political context in a manner that is appropriate for your children's age group.

How I Came Out to My 8 Year Old Son

I came out to my eight year old son when I brought my girlfriend home for the first time. We had been out bowling that day and we were all happy and relaxed. That evening, at bedtime while he brushed his teeth, I said, "Mike, I want you to know that Chris is more than Mom's friend, she's my girlfriend."

Mike looked at me and said, "You mean you kiss her?"

I said, "Yes."

Then he said, "You mean on the lips?"

I said "Yes, sometimes."

He proceeded to make sounds, "Ohooo yuck!

Then he said, "Let me see it Mom?"

"See what?" I asked.

"I want to see you kiss her on the lips."

He caught me by surprise. At first, I wasn't sure if I should. Then I realized he needed to see me kiss her on the lips, as a man would kiss a woman, to understand that she was really my girlfriend. Once we came out of the bathroom, I asked Chris to kiss me in front of him. We gave each other a quick peck on the lips and then I heard him scream "Uuuuhhhhh!" He then started to laugh. After that, we continued preparing dinner. It was a fun coming out experience, which we all look back at fondly.

Coming Out to Your Parents

There are many reasons why you should come out as a lesbian or bisexual to your parents, the main one being that you want to have an honest and truthful connection with them. After all, they are the people responsible for giving you life and for looking after you as you grew up. Shouldn't they know who you really are? For many women, it's the fear of being rejected and disappointing their parents that is at the root of staying closeted.

Chris's Coming Out Story to Her Parents

Growing up gay in a small town made my high school years excruciating. I was regularly taunted by other kids because they thought I was gay. After graduating high school, I chose to go to Toronto to escape the oppression I felt living there. Once there, I quickly made friends with other like-minded individuals. After being away from home for a few months, my parents continued to ask if I had a boyfriend or if I was interested in anyone. I didn't want to lie to them, so the next weekend I made up my mind to tell them that I was gay.

I went out to dinner with my Dad first. Over dessert, I told him I wasn't going to marry a man or have a family because I was gay. He grabbed my hand and said, "That's ok, we love you anyway." He has never been anything other than supportive. I asked him not to tell my Mom, because I wanted to tell her myself.

The following day, I went out with my Mom and told her the same thing. She however, had more questions than my Dad. She asked me, if I was sure? "How did I know"? "Had I been with anyone?"-"What did lesbians do together?" What about AIDS?"

After answering her questions, I felt she was still a bit confused but I knew she loved me regardless. Since then, my parents have met all of my serious girlfriends and we have a wonderful relationship today.

Here are some reasons you may be holding back:

- Fear that you'll be ostracized by your family.

- Fear that they will make you feel ashamed.

- Fear that they'll reject you and never want to see you again.

- Fear that you'll lose their love.

- Fear that they'll reject your partner.

- Fear that they'll reject your children.

- Fear that they'll kick you out of their house.

- Fear that they'll remove you from

their Will and Testament.

Fear, fear, FEAR! Don't let fear be the guiding force in making your decisions. Often it's not as bad as it may seem. Today, with the legalization of same-sex marriage in many countries, same-sex relationships are becoming more accepted. According to UC Davis, a Social Psychologist, "For heterosexuals, finding out that a loved one is gay may be a big surprise. It forces them to change their expectations. They need time, information and understanding."

After all, they too will need to go through a sort of coming out process, going from feelings of shock, to denial, to eventual acceptance. Most parents do accept their children; it may just take a bit of time.

Here are some reasons to come out to your parents:

- To be honest with them .

So you're not burdened with secrets.

- Because they keep asking you about dating men.

- Because they keep hinting that they want to see you married.

- Because they want grandchildren.

- Because they want to know why you broke up with your boyfriend.

- Because they want to know why you're not married.

- Because you want them to treat your girlfriend as a "real" girlfriend.
- Because you want them to be grandparents to your children .

- Because you want them to respect your lesbian relationship as a legitimate relationship .

Because you love them and believe they deserve to know the truth.

- Because you don't want to lie to them directly or through omission.

- Because you want them to come to your lesbian wedding.

Although your sexual orientation is a crucial part of who you are and is central in the formation of your identity, it is not entirely who you are. You may be a loving and sympathetic person, an artistic individual, an intellectual guru and a loyal and caring friend. All these roles define who you are. Your orientation is just another facet of your whole self. If kept hidden, those repressed feelings can escalate, enveloping your thoughts and consuming your days and devouring every bit of creative energy you have.

By coming out to your parents, you are essentially giving them the opportunity to accept you. If you do not come out to them, you won't know how they will react. People often feel a burden has been lifted off their shoulders once they've been open with their parents. Many claim to develop a new closeness and gain greater respect from them.

Deciding to come out is your first step. Once the decision is made, the act is halfway completed. Now you just need to take the physical steps to do so. The following are suggestions you could consider:

Preparation:

Think about possible reactions your parents may have when you come out to them. Create a list of these reactions and write a favorable solution for each one of them.

For example write:
"If I tell them I'm a lesbian...."

Dad will say:

"What about grandchildren?"

I will say:
- "I can still have children one day, if I choose."
- "I can adopt, inseminate."
- "I don't want to have children."

Mom will say:
"Why are you a lesbian, do you want to be a man?"

I will say:
- "I don't want to be a man, I just don't want a boyfriend."

- "I love being a woman."

- "Women who feel they are men or men who feel they are women are called transgendered."
- "Women who love women are called lesbians."

Use the following chart to draw out

some other potential scenarios.

I'll say, Mom, Dad, I'm a lesbian...

They'll say...	My Response...

Brainstorm these questions and any other scenarios you imagine for a few nights and always try to write a positive solution. The more prepared you feel the more confident you'll be when you do come out to them. If you present yourself in a confident manner, they'll feel your strength and likely accept you. If you come across as not being proud of who you are by expressing feelings of shame, they may sense that and express a similar sentiment.

I.   <u>The Direct Approach</u>

Some women wonder if they should come out to their parents, one at a time or to both simultaneously. This is a personal decision that you will need to make based on your comfort level and on the personality of your parents.

Here are two direct approaches: the group and the individual.

The Group Approach

Come out to your parents after dinner, when they are relaxed. Before dinner may not be a good time because you and your parents may be hungry and not in the best of moods. Furthermore, your coming out news may upset them and affect the enjoyment of the meal. After dinner or during dessert is a better time to come out. You and your parents will not be hungry and will be more relaxed when discussing your coming out topic.

Encourage them to ask questions. If they don't have any, pose some yourself and then proceed to answer them. Make references to famous people who are lesbians and who are out and proud. Tell them how you came to the realization that you are a lesbian or bisexual. Tell them if you are currently dating a woman. If they do not want to talk about the issue, accept their response and give them the time they need to come to terms with the news you have given them.

Make sure you have friends to support you throughout this process.

How I Came Out to My Mother

I came out to my Mom on Christmas Eve. I had been thinking about coming out to her for a while because I wanted to introduce her to my girlfriend. I was a bit sensitive that evening because it was Christmas and my girlfriend wasn't there. I was in the kitchen with my Mom preparing the meal when she asked, for what seemed like the millionth time, why I broke up with my boyfriend. Frustrated, I blurted out "Because, I'm gay!" She looked at me in disbelief and thought I was lying. I told her no, that it was the truth and that I had a girlfriend. When she realized I was telling the truth, she ran off to her bedroom and cried. I didn't know what to do, so I joined her in the bedroom. I sat beside her and told her my coming out story. How I had felt so depressed in the past and even thought about suicide. This made her pause and begin to ask questions.

She was eventually able to compose herself and complete dinner. We didn't talk about the issue for three months until one day she said I could bring my "special friend" to a family dinner. I was delighted! My Mom and I are much closer now than we have ever been.

The Individual Approach

If you decide to come out to each parent individually, do it over coffee or tea making sure you're both relaxed and calm. Coming out to one parent at a time ensures that you have their individual attention. It's important that they each have the freedom and privacy to react in the manner they choose. Some parents express anger. Others cry. Many just smile and accept. They will also have one-on-one time with you to ask any questions they may have without feeling embarrassed, hesitant or censored by the other parent.

II.　The Indirect Approach

Due to cultural or religious beliefs, some women prefer not to tell their parents that they are lesbian or bisexual directly, but rather, indirectly. They incorporate LGBT activities into their lives, such as attending Pride events, lesbian marches and LGBT BBQs. Sometimes, they will bring their girlfriends to family events without verbally saying to their parents that they are in a lesbian relationship. These women feel that their parents don't want to know directly, but will know from all the evidence around them. However, in these scenarios, there will always be an underlying silence and uncertainty as to whether their parents have really accepted them.

The following are three other indirect approaches to coming out to your parents:

Write a Letter

The first indirect method of coming out to your parents is to write them a letter. The art of writing a letter by hand can make a very personal and profound statement. Email tends to be less personal and you may not ever know if it was read by the person who received it. Your parent may not even see the email, depending on the security filters and volume of mail they have in their inbox. The act of writing by hand shows that you care and have taken the time to write something that is very important to you.

This method will also allow them time to process the information you sent, before responding to you. With a letter, you can share a great deal about yourself, how you feel and why you have decided to come out to them. You may want to tell them how much you love and respect them. In this way, you will not be interrupted or sidetracked as you come out to them. You will be less nervous using this method as you can shred the letter and re-write it as many times as you like.

Give them the letter when you feel the time is right for you. Try to be close by when they receive the letter, so they can speak to you immediately, if they choose. If you can't be nearby, let them know how you'd like to be reached. A letter is a very effective and non-confrontational method of coming out.

Henrietta's Story

I came from a strict European Catholic family, so coming out for me was very stressful. For years I wanted to tell my parents that I was in a loving relationship with a woman, but never had the courage to tell them. Family functions didn't include my partner and I had to exclude her from all conversations. My parents thought I was single and tried to set me up with men. Because I felt pressured, I eventually left home and moved to another country to avoid coming out to them. The distance made me miss them and the desire to be open with them grew stronger. In the end, I decided to come out to them by writing a series of letters. First, I wrote to my mother, then to my sister, and finally to my father. Their responses were so amazing that to this day, I'm overwhelmed with emotion.

My Mom responded quickly, asking me all kinds of questions. She said she loved me and missed me and begged me to return. My sister said that I shouldn't have run away because of that. My father just said it was ok, that I was still welcomed in the home. A year later, I returned home to my parent's warm embrace. I am so proud of them and I feel so lucky!

Give a Book

The second indirect approach is to give them a non-fiction book that addresses lesbianism (or homosexuality) from a historical, political or social perspective. For example, offer them the book: Coming out to Parents: Two-Way Survival Guide for Lesbians and Gay Men and Their Parents by Mary Borhek. If you feel your parents won't read a whole book on the topic, consider offering them a PFLAG brochure. Many of their brochures are very informative and list important resources, such as support groups, events, and useful phone numbers.

When offering your parents a book, it is a good idea to attach a note stating, "This is who I am." You could also add, "I love you. Please come talk to me whenever you're ready. I'll be happy to answer any questions," and wait for their reaction.

In this manner, you won't have to worry about directly confronting them or not having control over what you're going to say. Your parents will have the chance to absorb your announcement, educate themselves on the topic and approach you when it feels right to them.

Conversely, if you suspect that your parents will never approach you to discuss the issue, then you may need to just introduce your girlfriend to them one day; perhaps during a family event, in the most natural way possible. Even if the issue is never directly discussed by you and your parents, the truth will be out and there will be no more hiding your sexual orientation.

Ask a Family Member

Lastly, you could ask a family member to 'out' you to your parents; for example, ask your brother or sister to tell them. Some people ask their mothers to tell their fathers, or vice versa. The risk with this method is that you can't control how the information is conveyed to them.

Assure your family member that you will not blame him or her for 'outing' you or for any negative consequences that may arise. This is a lot to ask of another person and you may want to show your appreciation in some way for the actions they will be taking on your behalf.

Whatever method you choose, direct or indirect, make sure that you explain to your parents why you are coming out to them. It is important that you do it for the right reasons (not for spite or revenge); it should be because you care about them and value your relationship with them. Encourage them to ask you questions and engage them in as much positive dialogue as possible. Be patient, and let them come to terms with accepting you at their own time and pace. If you come out to your parents with respect and love, they will likely respond in a similar way to you. Don't forget, they love you; it's in their nature.

Parenting Questions

Occasionally, misguided questions are asked about how lesbian and gay parents affect the development of their children. Here are some common questions:

1. *Will children of lesbian/gay or bisexual parents have difficulty making friends?*

   Research conducted by the American Psychological Association (2008) indicates that children of lesbian (or gay) parents have normal social relationships with their friends and adults.

2. *Are they likely to be abused sexually, physically by a parent, or by the parent's friends?*

   Once again, the evidence states that there is no relationship between abuse and a lesbian/bi (or gay) household. The concerns raised regarding this issue are grounded in prejudice and stereotypes concerning gays and lesbians. Research indicates that children of homosexual households do not differ in their development from children of heterosexual households.

3. *Do children of lesbians or gays have more difficulty with issues regarding gender identity or gender roles?*

Research indicates that gender and sexual identities develop in the same way among children of heterosexual mothers as they do among lesbian mothers.

4. *Are children of lesbians more likely to develop mental and behavioural problems? Are they more psychologically vulnerable?*

Studies focusing on personality, self-identity and behavioural problems show no differences between children raised by lesbians and gays and children raised by heterosexual families.

Coming Out to Your Siblings

Coming out to your siblings can be similar to coming out to your friends or parents. Choose your method and believe that whatever the results, it will be for the best. Some siblings are very conservative and may struggle with accepting their gay brother or sister; others are very open-minded and probably already suspect that they have a lesbian or bisexual family member. You may already have a sense of how they'll respond. If you are unsure of how they will react, have an open discussion with them involving a lesbian event or news story. This should allow you to gauge how they feel about homosexuality.

Some women don't want to come out to their brother or sister because they fear they will be outed to their parents or extended family. Although you can ask your sibling to be respectful and not 'out' you before you are ready, this does not always occur. Coming out to your siblings shows that you have self-respect, and that you will not hide and lie about your life. It also communicates that you trust and care about them, and want only to foster a healthy relationship with them.

How I Came Out to My Sister

When I came out to my sister Pam, I told her, "You know I'm a lesbian, that's why I don't date guys." She just looked at me and walked away. Months later I mentioned it again and she responded with, "No you're not!" and walked away again. Luckily, I had joined a coming out group and had many friends to help me through this difficult time. I felt hurt that my sister couldn't accept who I really was.

Prior to telling her, I had already come out to my brother, and he accepted me with open arms, hugging me and telling me how he would love and respect me forever. However, it took my sister years to accept me for who I am. For a long time, she was silent and never inquired about my personal life. Today however, she is very accepting and I no longer feel judged by her.

Coming Out to Your Boyfriend or Husband

Many women find themselves in the awkward situation in which they are in relationships with men but fantasize about being with women. If you are in this situation, these feelings and your attraction towards women can be hauntingly persistent and self-tormenting if left unexplored.

Here are a few reasons women don't come out to their boyfriends or husbands:

- Fear of being shunned by their family.
- Fear of losing their home.
- Fear of losing their children.
- Fear of traumatizing their children.
- Fear of losing their financial support.
- Fear of rejection.
- Fear of violence.

- Fear of being lonely.
- Fear of hurting his feelings.

Coming out to your boyfriend or husband comes with its own set of risks. If you fear aggression or violence, make arrangements to find a safe place to stay, such as at a friend or family member's home or at a women's shelter. Ensure that you are surrounded by people that care about you and accept you as you are. If you have children, make sure they are in a safe place prior to coming out to your boyfriend or husband. Your safety and the safety of your children is a priority. Come out to him only if you feel it will benefit you more than it will harm you. If your boyfriend or husband has violent tendencies, it's best not to tell him and to leave him as soon as you can.

In more common situations, some men don't take a woman's coming out very seriously. Others think it is a fun and exciting idea. However, when their relationship begins to fall apart because their wife or girlfriend is interested in another woman, putting their relationship in jeopardy, the situation becomes more dramatic and potentially painful. On the other hand, your boyfriend or husband may decide to stay by your side and support you through your explorative process. You may want to stay in the relationship because you identify as bisexual. Regardless, make up your mind as to what role you want him to play in your life. Simply making this decision will make you feel more relaxed.

Here are some of the reasons to come out to your boyfriend or husband:

- You want to be honest with him.
- You want to end the relationship.
- You want to explore dating women.
- You want his support and friendship as you come out.
- You don't want to live a lie.
- You want your children to be raised

with honesty and love.
- You want to be in a relationship with a woman.

Honesty in a relationship is crucial to being happy and balanced. Relationships with secrets always suffer in the long run and often lead to separation or divorce.

Once you've made the decision to come out to him, your next step is to actually do it. The following suggested steps can be as varied as the people taking them; always do what feels right to you.

Discuss the Topic

If you don't know how your boyfriend or husband feels about homosexuality, engage him in a conversation on the topic to gauge his reaction. If you have been in the relationship for a while, you will likely know how he feels about the topic. Often straight men who haven't had much interaction with lesbians will say things like, "They're hot" (if they've seen too many porn movies) or that they (lesbians) are all butches.

Regardless, take the opportunity to make it real. Talk about prominent lesbians such as Jane Lynch, Rosie O'Donnell, Ellen DeGeneres and Portia de Rossi. This will focus the topic rather than speaking in general terms.

Coming Out to Him

Invite your boyfriend or husband out to dinner, or to go for a walk with you in a local park. A public place will be conducive to him staying calm and listening to you. If you have children, arrange childcare, as you don't want the children interrupting your conversation. What is important is that you are alone and in a positive frame of mind.

Whenever you feel comfortable, let him know that you have something very important to share. You may do this by handing him a letter which you prepared beforehand, or by just saying it all verbally.

Regardless, state your reasons for giving him this news. For instance you feel the need to be honest with him. You have something unsettling within you which needs to be explored. Or you're not sure of your future together as a couple.

If you're uncertain of what label you should apply to yourself, let him know that. If you're comfortable saying you're a lesbian, go for it. Some women are comfortable saying they are attracted to women or fantasize about them, but aren't sure if they're lesbian or bisexual. Other women prefer to simply say their gay.

Sometimes, boyfriends or husbands are excited by the prospect of lesbianism and its potential for a threesome. You will need to be clear that coming out is not meant to be a sexual adventure for him *(unless you want it to be)*. You may want to suggest that he seek outside support, for example, refer him to Matt Fried's website: GuideSpot.com, or to your local LGBT community centre where information and support groups may be available to help men in his situation.

Ultimately, he's going to have to cope on his own. Encourage him to seek out a close friend in whom he can confide. Your main responsibility is to be honest with him and to look after yourself. Carrying on in a relationship with secrets is emotionally and mentally taxing to both parties. Honesty and sincerity will be your best path.

Ensure You Have Adequate Support

Every man is different when it comes to responding to his girlfriend's or wife's coming out news. It is best if you are prepared to accept any reaction. Speak to a friend, preferably a gay or lesbian friend who can help you entertain all possible scenarios. Your friend may act as a devil's advocate in role-playing your boyfriend's potential reactions.

If you don't have any gay, lesbian or bisexual friends, you may want to join a coming out group at your local LGBT community centre. It is important that you surround yourself with positive people and find information to help you sort out how you feel. Join an online forum where lesbians and bisexual women gather to meet. Look for posts where they are talking about their relationships with men. Create your own post and wait for them to respond to you. You may be surprised to learn how similar your situations are, and how supportive and friendly people online can be.

Coming Out to My Boyfriend

I had a boyfriend for three years. His name was Joe. We were the perfect couple, at least to everyone around us. We talked about getting married and everything seemed to be going in that direction. There was only one problem; I kept thinking about girls and wanting to touch them. I felt this desire since I was a teenager, but always dismissed it. I was losing sleep because I was concerned that marriage was going to be a mistake for me.

More and more I felt like a sister towards him, and was compelled to tell him what I was feeling. One day, when I started crying he didn't understand what the problem was. Then, I told him that I didn't want to get married and that I thought I was a lesbian. He reacted with sympathy and said he'd be there to support me and that he loved me. He behaved the same way when a few years back I told him I had thyroid cancer. It seemed to me that this news had a similar impact on him. It was hard for him to accept that it was over between the two of us.

Weeks later, we were still walking hand in hand down the street as if nothing had changed. However, I was meeting new people; I was changing. I had joined a lesbian coming out group and had met a girl that I was interested in. Eventually he met my girlfriend and he and I drifted apart. It was a difficult time for him, but he did recover and married a few years later.

Coming Out to Your Child's Teacher

There are many reasons to come out to your child's teacher. First, it may be necessary in order to ensure that your child has a safe and productive school year. In most schools, a heterosexual nuclear family is still assumed. It's important to come out to the teacher for purposes of clarification; he or she may be very open to accepting lesbian or gay parents.

Second, it's important to ensure that your child is protected from bullying as a result of homophobia. Bullying may occur because your child's friends learned that he or she has two moms, or because he has no dad, or was adopted, or was conceived through artificial insemination from an anonymous donor. These and other scenarios may arise and you want your child's teacher to be prepared to handle them.

Finally, when class projects are assigned that involve some representation of a family, your child should be able to depict what is normal to him or her. If the teacher is aware of your child's unique family situation, this will help avoid confusion on Mother's or Father's Day. Your child could then be presented with an alternative such as create cards for: My Two Moms, My Favourite Aunt, or whatever is appropriate for your child.

Coming Out to the Teacher and Making Your Requests

This process can be as simple or as complicated as you choose. Some women will choose to bring their partners to meet the teacher on parent/teacher night, and introduce them as their significant other in a nonchalant manner. This method treats your family situation as normal and sets the expectation that it should be accepted as such. If you don't feel that this method is right for you, ask for a meeting with the teacher to explain the nuances of your family.

Prior to speaking to the teacher, it's advisable that you research the school's policy on lesbian and gay inclusion. It's a good idea to do this even before you choose a school; this way you ensure that your child has a safe and inclusive school experience.

Joint Custody

If there is a Dad involved in your child's upbringing, explain to the teacher the extent of his involvement in your child's life:

- Does the Dad have rights to drop off or pick up your child from school?

- Will the Dad be coming to parent teacher night?

- Will the Dad's consent be needed to

allow your child to participate in certain activities?

Sole Custody

• Explain that your child does not have a Dad.

• That any references to 'Dad' should be omitted or substituted with whatever makes sense to you (uncle, aunt or your partner).

Bullying

Express a concern to your child's teacher if you believe that your child is being bullied as a result of having lesbian/gay parents.

Make the following suggestions to increase awareness and acceptance:

• Request a zero tolerance approach in the classroom and on the school grounds regarding lesbian or gay discrimination

- State that LGBT slurs, jokes or teasing should not be permitted.

- Ask the teacher to read stories to the class that depict children with lesbian or gay parents such as: Heather Has Two Mommies.

- Suggest lesbian or gay speakers, (possibly yourself) to come to the classroom and talk about their families.

My Son's Homophobia

One day my son came home and said, "Mom, I think two women kissing is disgusting." I was appalled. He had seen my partner and I kiss many times, but never said anything like that. He said that it wasn't right for two women to get married. I asked him who said that and he said, "My friends from school." We tried not to make a big deal of it, but knew something had to be done, so we made an appointment to meet with the teacher. We introduced ourselves as Mike's mothers and said we were concerned about his recent comments at home. The teacher was very understanding and said she would talk to the class about what is appropriate and non-appropriate behaviour. I also lent her a children's book I've had for years entitled: Ash's Mums. She accepted the book and said she'd read it to the class. We didn't have any problems after that.

Coming Out at Work

Many people feel there is no need to come out at work, believing that what they do in the privacy of their own bedroom is their business. However, it's not always so simple. For many, their work is a significant part of their lives. Most people spend a minimum of 8 hours at work daily, and that's at least 40 hours per week or 160 per month. Work is where their main social connections are made. It's an environment filled with all sorts of human interactions, conflicts, laughter and of course, gossip. If you are not out to your colleagues, you may feel left out, unheard, insulted and most of the time closeted!

Silence on your part can lead your colleagues to become suspicious and may even alienate you. Questions like, "What did you do this weekend?" can become stressful and lead you to lie or avoid contributing to the conversation.

Your silence can also be harmful to your physical and mental wellbeing; denying your true self and not sharing what you feel can lead to stress and even physical ailment. A study published June 2011 in Social Psychology and Personality Science showed that the benefits of revealing one's sexual identity leads to less anger, less depression and higher self-esteem. However, these positive experiences are limited to supportive settings[4].

First, Do Some Homework!

Before coming out to a work colleague, research your company's policies on lesbian and gay rights in the workplace. Is there an anti-discrimination policy? If yes, then you know you're backed up legally. If not, proceed with extreme caution, as in some countries, coming out is not safe or advisable. Unfortunately, some countries such as

---

[4] ScienceDaily (June 20, 2011)

the US, allow employers to terminate an employee for merely being gay or lesbian. In Canada, Sweden, Belgium, the Netherlands, and in many other countries, there are laws against discrimination because of sexual orientation.[5] In fact, many workplaces support LGBT rights and offer same-sex family benefits. If you do decide to come out at work, make sure you have done your homework first so you do not put yourself at risk.

Choosing a Colleague

If you know someone at the office who is gay or lesbian, this would be a good person to approach for advice. You may

---

[5] State recognition of same-sex couples: The Netherlands, Belgium, Canada, South Africa, Spain, Norway, Sweden, Portugal, Iceland, Argentina; U.S. states of Massachusetts, Connecticut, Iowa, Vermont, New Hampshire, New York, and the District of Columbia; most all European nations; New Zealand and Uruguay. Wikipedia

not know them very well, but having your sexual orientation in common may be enough to bond you and create a place of safety and support at work. If you don't know another lesbian, bisexual or gay person, you may want to come out to a trusted colleague.

When choosing someone to come out to at work, take your time, study several people, and observe their interactions. For example, do they make homophobic remarks? Do they speak using inclusive terms such as "partner"? Engage this person in a discussion about a famous lesbian or gay person. Listen to how he or she speaks. Is it a favorable viewpoint? If not, they will likely not be receptive to your coming out news. It may be best to approach someone else. When you find a person who has replied favourably to your queries, the chances are high that they will accept you.

When deciding to come out to your colleague, consider the following questions:

- What do I have to lose by coming out to this person?
- What do I have to gain?
- What are the risks involved?
- Will I lose my job? Get demoted? Get promoted? Or stay the same?

Do not make a hasty decision. A good rule of thumb is to choose the person you feel closest to, the person you feel understands you best and has proven to be supportive to you from past work experiences.

How to Come Out to Your Colleague

Coming out to a colleague at work can be as easy as mentioning: *"My partner Laura and I went away on the weekend."* Your co-worker will likely ask you follow-up questions. It doesn't need to be complicated.

Coming out to your colleagues shows that you trust and believe in them. You can ask them directly not to 'out' you because it's really your personal decision to whom you tell and when. However, once you've told someone, it's no longer a secret. Your best option is to hold your head high and not show any vulnerability. This will demonstrate that you have self-respect and nothing to hide. Gossip will stop if there is no secret to be kept hidden.

After coming out to a colleague successfully, you may decide to repeat the process. However, just coming out to at least one person at work will be an important step towards feeling better in the workplace and feeling more relaxed.

How I Came Out at Work

For a long time, I felt closeted at work. When my colleagues asked me about my weekend, I would omit my partner from the conversation all together. I'd say my friends and I did this or that, but in fact, it was just her and I. Sometimes, I'd say I did nothing just so I wouldn't have to lie. I kept quiet most of the time.

When my partner and I became more serious and we moved in together, I knew I couldn't stay closeted much longer. One day when talking to my colleague Marta about my upcoming vacation, I told her, "I'm going with my son and girlfriend." At first she didn't get it. I had to clarify by saying that my girlfriend and I were living together, as partners. She still didn't seem to get it, so I said, "I'm a lesbian." She was surprised, but took it well. She actually congratulated me for coming out to her and said I had a lot of courage. I'm not sure if she told anyone else at work. I didn't ask her to keep it a secret, but everything has been fine at work. The only difference is that some of my work colleagues seem to take more notice of me and they seem friendlier. I'm not sure if she 'outed' me, but if this is the result, then I don't mind at all. Now I just assume everyone knows I am a lesbian, so I speak truthfully when asked about my weekend or vacation plans. I do not omit my partner; rather, I include her in every answer.

Coming Out to Your Health Care Provider

It is vital that your health care provider knows about your sexual orientation to ensure that you are receiving the best health care service available. It's also very uncomfortable to be hiding your orientation, past sexual experiences and current relationships during a routine medical visit. Not only is it personally troubling, it can be unsafe, as your healthcare practitioner will not have all the information to make a proper diagnosis regarding your health problems. Your medical record should be complete so other health care practitioners or specialists can view it in the future. In that way, you do not have to continue coming out to each practitioner.

Here are some additional reasons to come out to your health care practitioner:

- To ensure all possible and appropriate treatment options are available to you.

- To make sure you are presented with accurate alternative treatment techniques, such as artificial insemination and surrogate birth.

- So you are not assumed to be heterosexual.

- To ascertain that your medical history is accurate.

It is important to shop around for an LGBT positive clinic. In many North American cities there are specific LGBT clinics; look for listings in your local phone directory.

Coming Out to Your Practitioner

Usually, on a first visit, a doctor will ask if you are sexually active. At this point, you can elaborate saying something to the effect of "Yes, I have sex with women," and "Yes, I'm in a long-term relationship with a woman" or, "I'm bisexual; I have had sex with both men and women". If your practitioner seems to be uncomfortable with your disclosure and is hesitant to treat you, it may be best to seek another professional.

Once you are out to your practitioner and have been accepted in a way that makes you feel comfortable, you will most likely feel relieved and relaxed discussing any concerns you may have. From that point on when you visit your practitioner, you can just be yourself. In this way, you should be receiving the best possible service the healthcare sector has to offer.

In some regions, discrimination against the LGBT community is still prevalent. In Canada, as in many other countries, it is illegal to discriminate based on sexual orientation. If you do decide to come out to your health care provider, make sure you have researched the rights you have as a member of the LGBT community in your province, state or region to ensure you receive adequate health care.

How I Came Out to My Doctor

For many years I wasn't out to my family doctor. I just didn't see him often enough and I didn't feel he needed to know. I questioned how open-minded he was and couldn't see the benefit of coming out to him. When I stopped having my period, I went through many tests. When we discussed the results, he asked me if I had a boyfriend and if I wanted to have children. I told him that I was a lesbian and I wasn't sure if I wanted children. He only paused for a second and then continued to explain that I couldn't have children naturally. Although I hadn't planned it, I was relieved that my being a lesbian was out in the open.

One day during a routine visit, he asked me about my coming out process. I was unclear why he took such a sudden interest in learning the details of my coming out story, but I gladly shared it with him. He said that he was writing an article on the issue of youth coming out to their parents, and if I would be interested in helping him out. He asked me if I knew anyone else who would share their story, and I said I would put together a lesbian/gay panel. He was delighted and included all their stories in his article. He would later go on to publish a book entitled: So Your Child is Gay (Dr. Jerald Bain).

Coming Out to Your Local Politician

Many lesbian and bisexual women believe it's important to come out to their local politician because they feel the need to raise awareness, bring about more acceptance, lessen discrimination, and in general create greater equality across the LGBT community and society as a whole. Coming out to your politician makes them aware of the number of LGBT individuals in their constituency as well as their need for equality. In many US states, same-sex marriage and civil unions are prohibited, as are same-sex adoptions.

It is crucial that you know your local politician's views on LGBT issues so you can decide if you will be supporting them at election time. They are appointed officials who have the mission to support and help their constituents live in safe communities free of discrimination. If they are not representing you and working towards fairness and equality for all, are they really doing their jobs? If they show a bias against you or your family because of their own personal prejudices, then they should know they will lose your vote.

If you decide to speak to your local politician, ensure you are clear about the reasons why you want to come out to him or her. It is best to do a bit of research about your politician first by taking a look at their website and newsletter. Take note of their political stance on homosexuality; do they accept, tolerate or discriminate? What's their voting history on supporting same-sex bills or policies?

Most politicians will see their constituents by appointment. If you have difficulty reaching them, keep insisting and you should be able to talk to them eventually. Make sure that you have a clear goal in your mind as far as what you want to accomplish. For example, you may want to bring a signed petition to illustrate that you represent a larger group of people who want same-sex couples to have equal rights, specifically when it comes to marriage and adoption. By sharing your own personal struggles and experiences regarding same-sex discrimination, you will give your politician a real sense of how inequality affects the LGBT community and their families. It is good to come prepared with questions. Here are some key questions to ask your local politician:

- How do you define a family?

- Do you support same-sex relationships?

- Are you in favour of same-sex marriages?

- How do you feel about lesbians and gays adopting children?

- How do you feel about lesbians and gays having children?

- How would you address bullying or discrimination in schools related to homophobia?

- How have you voted on same-sex bills in the past?

- Would you support a bill that accepts same-sex marriages and adoption rights?

Instead of meeting privately with your local politician, you can choose to take advantage of public forums where they will be speaking live. In these public forums, your local politician has nowhere to hide and will have to answer your questions truthfully and directly. The audience will also have the benefit of hearing his or her political stance on LGBT issues.

Regardless of how your local politician responds, what is vital is that you have been vocal and have brought greater public visibility to the issues that matter to you. In the end, the answers given by your local politician will reveal if he or she is worthy of your ongoing support.

My Political Action Story

When I was the facilitator of a lesbian support group, we decided to write a letter to our local MP (Minister of Parliament) to point out that the LGBT community needed equal rights and same-sex marriages. Together, we wrote a letter and obtained over 1,220 names (gathered during Pride Day) and sent it off to the MP's office.

A few weeks later we followed up. We learned from the receptionist that the letter had disappeared. Fortunately, we had the original letter and this time we asked to speak directly to the MP. Eventually, we did meet with him personally and presented him our letter with all the signatures on it. He read it in front of us and said that he would make sure our concerns were heard in Parliament. However, we discovered that he did not advocate on our behalf and as a result he lost our support and the support of many of the women who signed the petition.

Coming Out at Church

Churches, or spiritual places, are in general important institutions in the lives of many lesbians and bisexual women. This is not only because they are important places of worship but because they provide people with the opportunity to foster meaningful social connections and gain a sense of community. Nevertheless, for many LGBT people, churches do not provide them with a feeling of safety. Through the mere omission of the words lesbian, gay, bisexual and homosexual during church services, the issue is kept silent and thus, invisible.

Coming out in your church means that you are not hiding your relationships and your family. Social events at church should be inclusive and you should feel comfortable taking your same-sex partner and children with you. If you do not feel included during church services or events, discuss it with your church leader.

If your church leader's position is based on scripture and the interpretation that homosexuality is morally wrong, then you are not welcome in that church. Consult the following websites to get a fuller understanding of what Christian scripture says about homosexuality, Christian Gays: christiangays.com. There are also some very good films: Fish Out of Water and For The Bible Tells Me So. These reveal that religious anti-gay bias is based solely upon a misinterpretation of the Bible.

There are LGBT friendly churches, synagogues, and other religious and spiritual spaces, especially in large cities; it is a question of finding one that accepts you and your family. Look online, under the key words "gay friendly _____" (name your church)" For a listing of

LGBT positive churches, consult the following: GayChurch. org.

Spirituality is a very important part of many people's lives. Churches are places where you can express that spirituality, though they are not the only places. You can simply pray on your own or with a group of selected friends.

Make sure that the spiritual place you find is open and accepting of who you are and hence, you are free to enjoy all the benefits of spiritual freedom.

My Experience with Religion

Since I was raised Catholic I attended church off and on. This was mainly due to the fact that I didn't feel very accepted by the church and its teachings. Nonetheless, I did feel the need to connect to an institution and to others for spiritual guidance. As a result, I began looking for another church. I was thrilled when I found the Metropolitan Community Church in Toronto; it welcomed me with open arms. The pastor was openly gay and his sermons struck a chord with the things that mattered to me. I met wonderful people there and have always felt a sense of solidarity and belonging.

Reducing Discrimination

As a lesbian or bisexual woman, you can minimize discrimination by being open about your own sexual orientation. It's important to find heterosexual allies because they can have tremendous influence on persuading other heterosexuals to be more accepting, as they will likely support inclusive sexual orientation policies. Once you come out, heterosexuals around you will have the opportunity to know a lesbian or a bisexual woman and will perceive you as an individual and not as a stereotype.

Studies of prejudice against lesbian and gays consistently indicate that discrimination declines when heterosexuals interact with homosexuals[6]. One of the most powerful influences on heterosexuals' acceptance is having personal contact with an openly gay person.

---

[6] *American Psychological Association. (2008).*

Secrecy

Once you decide to come out to the various people in your life, be prepared to have your secret exposed, one way or another. It is unfair to ask people you trust to carry your secret. It places an unnecessary burden on them. Secrets only serve to distance you from others; they make you vulnerable and weak. When others know you have a secret, they have power over you, which can in some cases be used against you. Why let that happen? It's your life, release your secret and empower yourself with pride and strength. After all, do we not all want and crave freedom, whether it is personal or social? Coming out will set you FREE!

Closing Remarks

Coming out means you are PROUD of who you are. It also means that you love and respect yourself and treasure the relationships you have nurtured over the course of your life. As an out lesbian or bisexual woman, you are showing the world what it means to be a proud and confident woman. This is true role modelling and activism at its best. It leads to   stronger people, healthier families and ultimately, more accepting and integrated societies.

I appreciate you purchasing this book and I wish you the best in your coming out journey. May your future endeavours be filled with love, joy and personal fulfillment.

I'd love to hear from you. I welcome your comments, opinions or questions. Please send them to:
howtocomeout@gmail.com

Glossary

Heterosexism

An assumption that heterosexuality is the only valid option and that every person should develop romantic, sexual relationships with people of the opposite sex.

Homophobia

Homophobia is literally defined as discrimination against presumed or overt homosexuals. In a work environment, homophobia can translate into behaviours (words, gestures or writing) and harassment that attack a person's dignity and integrity because he or she is homosexual or perceived as such.

Homophobic language

Homosexuals who internalize prejudice and homophobic social standards may even feel put down, come to hate themselves and in turn put down and hate homosexuals around them.

Insults, jokes, negative vocabulary that stigmatizes homosexuality and homosexuals.

Internalize Homophobia
Personal acceptance and endorsement of sexual stigma as part of the individual's value system and self-concept. It is the counterpart to sexual prejudice among heterosexuals (Herek, Gillis, & Cogan, 2009).

Personal Homophobia
Personal feelings or beliefs that homosexuals are abnormal, bizarre, or sick.

Social and Cultural Homophobia
Social and cultural standards favoring heterosexuals at the expense of homosexuals. Granting privileges

unconsciously. Social, cultural and religious values. Books, icons that exclude homosexuals.

Bibliography

1. Coming Out A Guide To Coming Out Of The Closet, by Ramon Johnson, About.com Guide

2. The University of Tennessee, Coming out: A Guide for Youth and Their Allies, by the Gay, Lesbian and Straight Education Network.

3. Coming Out Can Reduce Sexual Prejudice; Herek, G.M. (1997). Heterosexuals' attitudes toward lesbians and gay men: Does coming out make a difference? M. Duberman (Ed.), A queer world: The Centre for Lesbian and Gay Studies Reader, New York: New York University Press.

4. Coming Out: A Guide for Youth and Their Allies , GLSEN: Gay, Lesbian, and Straight Education Network, Jan 23, 2003.

5. Is Coming out Always a Good Thing? Disclosing Sexual

6. Orientation Makes People Happier Than Thought, but Mainly in Supportive Settings, Science Daily, Nicole Legate, Richard M. Ryan, Netta Weinstein

7. Parents Families & Friends of Lesbians & Gays (PFLAG), Bisexuality Resource Packet Talking About Homosexuality in the Secondary School, AVERT (1997)

8. People Coming Out as Gay at Younger Age, The Guardian, Rachel Williams, November 2010

9. Sexual Orientation and Psychotherapy, Phillips S, Richardson J & Vaughan S. Gabbard G, Beck J & Holmes J (2005), Oxford textbook of psychotherapy Oxford University Press: Oxford.

10. Six Stages to Coming Out, W Counselling Centre, University of Washington, The Cass Theory, developed by Vivian Cass (1979)

11. Wikipedia, Free Online Encyclopedia

Top 10 Lists

Lesbian Bi Resources

10 Coming Out Books

10 Lesbian Novels

10 Lesbian Erotica

10 Children's Books with a LGBT Theme

10 Teen Lesbian Books

10 Bisexuality Books

10 Lesbian/Bi Films

10 Lesbian/Bi Forums

10 Lesbian Dating Sites

10 Coming Out Books

1. Coming out and Disclosures: LGBT Persons Across the Life Span - Ski Hunter

2. Coming out to Parents: A Two-Way Survival Guide for Lesbians and Gay Men and Their Parents - Mary Borhek

3. Coming out: Telling Family and Friends (The Gallup's Guide to Modern Gay, Lesbian, & Transgender Lifestyle) - Jaime A. Seba

4. Family Outing: A Guide to the Coming-Out Process for Gays, Lesbians & Their Families - Chastity Bono and Billie Fitzpatrick

5. For Lesbian Parents: Your Guide to Helping Your Family Grow Up Happy, Healthy and Proud - Suzanne M. Johnson Phd and Elizabeth O'Connor Phd

6. Lesbian Epiphanies: Women Coming out in Later Life - John Dececco Phd and Karol L Jensen

7. Outing Yourself: How to Come Out as Lesbian or Gay to Your Family, Friends and Coworkers - Michelangelo Signorile

8. Redefining the Self: Coming out As Lesbian - Laura A. Markowe

9. Testimonies: Lesbian Coming-Out Stories - Sarah Holmes

10. The Other Side of the Closet: The Coming-Out Crisis for Straight Spouses and Families - Amity Buxton

10 Lesbian Novels

1. Affinity - Sarah Waters

2. Desert of the Heart - Jane Rule

3. Fingersmith - Sarah Waters

4. Fried Green Tomatoes at the Whistle Stop Café - Fannie Flagg

5. Oranges Are Not the Only Fruit - Jeanette Winterson

6. Ruby Fruit Jungle – Rita Mae Brown

7. Sing You Home - Jodi Picoult

8. The Hours - Michael Cunningham

9. The Sealed Letter - Emma Donoghue

10. Tipping the Velvet: A Novel - Sarah Waters

10 Lesbian Erotica

1. A Lesbian Bedtime Companion: Erotic Lesbian Short Stories - Jennifer Casey

2. After Midnight: True Lesbian Erotic Confessions –Chelsea James

3. Best Lesbian Erotica 2007 - Tristan Taormino

4. Best Lesbian Erotica 2011 - Kathleen Warnock

5. Best Lesbian Erotica 2011 - Kathleen Warnock and Lea DeLaria

6. Erotic Tales: Lesbian Encounters - Mythic Tales Publishing

7. Georgia's English Rose - J T Harding

8. Girls On Top: Explicit Erotica For Women - Violet Blue

9. She Slipped and Fell – Shonda

10. Where The Girls Are: Urban Lesbian Erotica - D L King

10 Children's Books with LGBT Theme

1. Asha's Mums - Rosamund Elwin

2. Emma and Meesha My Boy: A Two Mom Story - Kaitlyn Taylor Considine

3. Heather Has Two Mommies - Leslea Newman

4. Keesha & Her Two Moms Go Swimming - Monica Bey-Clarke and Cheril N. Clarke

5. King & King - Linda De Haan and Stern Nijland

6. Mommy, Mama, and Me - Leslea Newman

7. Pigeons Don't Float! - Jennifer C. Manion

8. The Rainbow Cub- House - Brenna and Vicki Harding

9. Who's in a Family - Robert Skutch

10. Yorkie Has 2 Moms and 2 Schnauzers - Getaway Hawayek Narbaitz

10 Teen Lesbian Books

1. Annie on My Mind - Nancy Garden

2. Dare Truth or Promise - Paula Boock

3. Empress of the World - Sara Ryan

4. GLBTQ: The Survival Guide for Gay, Lesbian, Bisexual, Transgender, and Questioning Teens - Kelly Huegel

5. Keeping You a Secret - Julie Anne Peters

6. Luna - Julie Anne Peters

7. Not the Only One: Lesbian and Gay Fiction for Teens - Jane Summer

8. Potential - Aerial Schrag

9. Sugar Rush - Julie Burchill's

10. Two Teenagers in 20: Writings - Gay and Lesbian Youth - Ann Heron

10 Bisexuality Books

1. Bi Any Name: Bisexual People Speak Out - Loraine Hutchins

2. Bisexual Resource Guide - Robyn Ochs

3. Bisexuality and the Eroticism of Everyday Life - Marjorie B. Garber

4. Bisexuality in the Ancient World - Eva Cantarella and Cormac OCuilleanain

5. Bisexuality in the United States - Paula C. Rodriguez Rust

6. Dare... to Try Bisexuality - Pierre Des Esseintes

7. Dual Attraction: Understanding Bisexuality - Martin S. Weinberg

8. Sexuality: The Psychology and Politics of an Invisible Minority - Beth A. Firestein

9. The Sex and Love Handbook... Kris A Heinlein and Rozz M Heinlein

10. Women and Bisexuality: A Global Perspective - Serena Anderlini D'Onofrio

10 Lesbian Coming out Films

1. But I'm a Cheerleader

2. Desert Hearts

3. Goldfish Memory

4. Imagine Me and You

5. Kissing Jessica Stein

6. Kissing Jessica Stein

7. Nina's Heavenly Delights

8. Saving Face

9. The Truth About Jane

10.   When Night is Falling

10 Lesbian/Bi Films

1. A Girl Thing

2. Better than Chocolate

3. Bound

4. Fingersmith

5. Gray Matters

6. It's in the Water

7. Loving Annabelle

8. Portrait of a Marriage

9. Saving Face

10. Tipping the Velvet

10 Lesbian/Bi Forums

1. About Com – Lesbian Life

2. Bella Online

3. Gay/Lesbian Forum

4. Hip Forum

5. LesbiansToday

6. Love Girls

7. Melswebs

8. Pink Sofa

9. Super Dyke

10. The L Chat

10 Dating Sites

1. Gay Girl Date

2. Gaydar Girls

3. Girls Parship

4. L Date

5. Lesbian Personals

6. Lesbian Romance

7. Metrodate

8. Pink Cupid

9. Pink Sofa

10. Planet Sappho

Other Resources

Canada

Kids help phone.ca
1 800-668-6868

Youth Line.ca
1 800 268-9688

Sexuality and U
This page has almost everything you need to know about sexual orientation and gender identity, from coming out to helping a friend and finding support.

http://sexualityandu.ca/en/sexual-health/sexual-identity-and-orientation

PFLAG Canada
PFLAG provides support, information and resources to gay, lesbian, bisexual, transgender or questioning people, as well as to their families and friends.
http://www.pflagcanada.ca/

Queer Asian Youth

This site is a space for gay, lesbian, bisexual, transsexual, transgender, queer, or questioning East and Southeast Asian youth, as well as their friends and families. Coming out resources are available in English, Chinese, Japanese, Korean and Tagalog.
http://www.qay.ca/index.php

Salaam: Queer Muslim Community

This site offers information and support to gay and lesbian people in the Muslim community. Information is also available on group meetings in Toronto, Halifax, and Vancouver.
http://www.salaamcanada.com/

The Cool Page for Queer Teens

This site offers help with questions like: Am I gay? and should I come out? You can also get information on talking to parents, dealing with harassment or discrimination, safer sex, and AIDS.
http://www.bidstrup.com/cooldat.htm

MyGSA.ca

This site provides info and resources for LGBTQ youth and allies looking to make Canadian schools discrimination-free. Connect with other young people; find scholarships, watch videos and more.
http://www.mygsa.ca/locker

Canada - Regional Pages

Regional pages may still have helpful resources for youth throughout Canada, but some of the services will only be available locally.

Lesbian Gay Bi Trans Youth Line (Ontario)

Youth Line is a peer-to-peer support line for lesbian, gay, bisexual, transgender, transsexual, two-spirited, queer and questioning youth across Ontario. Free and confidential support is available over the phone and online. http://www.youthline.ca/

Central Toronto Youth Services (Toronto)

Central Toronto Youth Services is a place where gay, lesbian, bisexual, intersex, trans,

and questioning youth can receive counselling and community support. Pride and prejudice programs are also available to youth under the age of 25.
http://www.ctys.org/

The 519 Church Street Community Centre (Toronto)
http://www.the519.org/
This Toronto community centre provides counselling and support to lesbian, gay, bisexual, transgender, transsexual and queer communities. Anti-poverty and homelessness programs and legal services are available for both youth and adults. Information for friends and families is also available.

HOPE -Haltonpride.org (Halton, Ontario)
Information on sexual orientation, plus support and networking opportunities for teenagers living in Halton region, Ontario.
http://www.haltonpride.org/

Germany

Gay Groups and Support Services in Germany

LSVD

Tel: 0221 925 96 10
Fax: 0221 9259 6111
http://berlin.angloinfo.com/information/32/gl.asp

International

ILGA – International Lesbian Gay Association
http://ilga.org/

UK

HELPLINE: 0300 330 0630
London gay and lesbian switchboard: 020 7837 7324
http://www.llgs.org.uk/

Domestic violence: Broken Rainbow

08452 60 44 60
http://www.broken-rainbow.org.uk/

Disabled LGBT: Regard
UK Counselling Support Network

http://www.counselling-directory.org.uk/

USA

GLBT NATIONAL HELP Centre
Serving the Gay, Lesbian, Bisexual and
Transgendered Community
1 888 843-4564

http://www.glbtnationalhelpcentre.org/find
/northeast.html

GLBT National Youth Talkline
1-800-246-7743

Gay & Lesbian National Hotline
1-888-THE-GLNH (1-888-843-4564)

Gay, Lesbian, Bisexual, and Transgender
(GLBT) Youth Support Line
800-850-8078

Gay & Transgender Hate Crime Hotline
1-800-616-HATE

Healing Woman Foundation (Abuse)
1-800-477-4111

Help Finding a Therapist
1-800-THERAPIST (1-800-843-7274)

Homeless/Runaway National Runaway Hotline
800-231-6946

Independent Adoption Centre
1-800-877-6736

Mental Health Info Source
1-800-447-4474

National Adoption Centre
1-877-648-4400

National Adolescent Suicide Hotline
800-621-4000

National Child Abuse Hotline
1-800-422-4453

National Domestic Violence Hotline
1-800-799-SAFE (1-800-799-7233)

National Drug Abuse Hotline
1-800-662-HELP (1-800-662-4357)

National Inhalant Prevention Coalition
1-800-269-4327

National Institute on Drug Abuse & Alcoholism
1-888-644-6432

National Institute of Mental Health
1-888-ANXIETY (1-888-269-4389)

National Mental Health Association
1-800-969-6642

National Runaway Switchboard and Suicide Hotline
1-800-621-4000

National Suicide Prevention Lifeline
1-800-273-TALK

National STD Hotline
1-800-227-8922

National Teen Dating Abuse Help
1-866-331-9474

National Youth Crisis Hotline
1-800-448-4663

National Victim Centre
1-800-FYI-CALL (1-800-394-2255)

About the Author

Essie Reis has a Bachelor of Arts Degree from the University of Toronto, specializing in Sociology and Psychology. She has worked extensively as a lesbian activist and LGBT counselor. She has chaired numerous gay and lesbian committees, co-founded a lesbian and gay multicultural association and has facilitated a number of coming out groups.

The author, welcomes your comments and questions. Please direct them to:
howtocomeout@gmail.com

Famous Lesbians
<u>Coming Out</u> Stories

<u>Chely Wright</u>

Excerpt from People Magazine - May 10, 2010

"Nothing in my life has been more magical than the moment I decided to come out…"

"I don't have a memory in my life that doesn't include the dream of making music." But during her childhood and rapid ascent to fame in the country world, she also experienced a community in which homosexuality was shunned. "I hid everything for my music," she said.

The country-music singer said that at one point she picked up a gun and was close to pulling the trigger – trapped as a closeted lesbian and afraid of losing everything in a conservative industry that might not accept who she really was.

"I had a 9-millimeter gun in my mouth," Chely said on the *Today* show. "I was living a secret life, and I was very much a country-music celebrity ... I gave up hope, and I was ready to take my own life."

The pressure had been building, she said, ever since John Rich of country-music duo Big & Rich asked her if she was gay – the first time she'd ever been asked directly after years of avoiding the issue.

She recalls: "John finally asked me point blank: You're not gay? If you are, people won't have it. It's sick, it's deviant, and it's unacceptable to country-music fans. You're not, are you? "

Chely said, "I lied. And I knew that I had gone from not talking about it to being a liar."

Chely Wright is also the author of a new memoir *Like Me: Confessions of a Heartland Country Singer*, admits she had some trepidation about how fans would react to her announcement. "I am not afraid," she says. "I'm not ashamed. And besides, a huge weight has been lifted. It feels incredible," she said. "I feel as if it's my birthday."

Chely's new book-Like Me

Ellen DeGeneres

Excerpt TIME, April 14, 1997 - On Being Closeted

"I hate that term 'in the closet,'"

"Until recently I hated the word lesbian too," she continues. "I've said it enough now that it doesn't bother me. But lesbian sounded like somebody with some kind of disease. I didn't

155

like that so I used the word gay more often.

"I always thought I could keep my personal life separate from my professional life in every interview I ever did" she continued " everyone tried to trap me into saying I was gay. And I learned every way to dodge that. Or if they just blatantly asked me, I would say I don't talk about my personal life. I mean, I really tried to figure out every way to avoid answering that question for as long as I could."

On Coming Out

"For me this has been the most freeing experience because people can't hurt me anymore. I don't have to worry about somebody saying something about me or a reporter trying to find out information. Literally, as soon as I made this decision, I lost weight. My skin has cleared up. I don't have anything to be scared of which I think outweighs whatever else happens in my career."

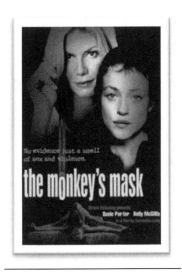

<u>Kelly McGillis</u>

Excerpts from the Internet Show "Girl Rock"

"I think that was an ongoing process from the time I was probably 12. It was a long arduous journey for me," she told the publication. "I had a lot of bad things happen to me that made me think God was punishing me for being gay. Life is a freaking journey about coming to terms

158

with who and what you are."

Excerpts from the Daily Mail.co.uk – by Paul Scott

The 53-year-old Kelly McGillis has gone public for the first time about her love for music company executive Melanie Leis, the on-off lover she has kept secret for the last nine years.

"I have no secrets anymore and in some ways it's a relief," the twice-married McGillis said this week after finally tying the knot with 42-year-old Leis.

It was not always the case. Until the ceremony last month, attended by just 11 friends, McGillis had steadfastly refused to acknowledge her relationship with Melanie Leis.

Now, with extraordinary courage, the publicity-shy star has admitted she hid her sexuality after becoming convinced she was being 'punished by God' for being gay.

It led, she says, to her falling into two disastrous marriages, and numbing the guilt over her secret life with years of alcoholism and drug-taking.

Now it seems, the once-tortured McGillis has finally found the happiness that has eluded her for so long.

KD Lang

Excerpt taken from Diva, July 2011

By the time she was five she knew the two things that would define her. She had a magnificent voice and she loved women. Her first crush was on an "athletic and gorgeous girl" she met as a tot, outside her father's drugstore. There was never any doubt. From age of 13 she was very active and had many girlfriends. "I came out to one of my sisters first, I was giving her a piggy-back around the living room. I had her up on my shoulders and we both said at the same time that we thought we were bisexual, because we didn't really know the word for it."

"I had been on a couple of dates with boys but I never had sex. I kissed them and I had sexual explorations with a boy. It wasn't that much different. It was just that it seemed more natural for me to be with girls."

When she came out to her mother at 17, it was hardly shocking. She is the youngest of three girls and one boy and only one of the girls is not gay. "I think I came out for the whole family. Then we all came out at the same time. It was difficult for my mother, but now she's totally cool."

KD Lang was born in Consort, a small Alberta town where, "you know all of them, you know their dog's names and who they're sleeping with. Everyone has got their quirks, so if anything, it made things easier, I never saw anything wrong with it (my sexuality)."

Meredith Baxter

Excerpts from an interview on Today, NBC, Dec 2009

Baxter told Matt Lauer "I am a lesbian and it was a later-in-life recognition." She said some people said that she had been living a lie, but in fact she only became aware that she was a lesbian in the past seven years. "I've always lived a very private life. To come out and disclose stuff is very antithetical to who I am."

To the question are you happy? Meredith answered: "I'm extraordinarily happy," she added that "I'm not a very political person …but it's been brought to my attention that this is a political act," she stated that research has revealed that if people know lesbians and gays personally they are more likely to support same sex equality and to vote for same sex rights. "So if you knew me before and you cared about me before, I'm the same woman, I'm the same mother to all these children."

Excerpt from People, Dec 2009

Meredith Baxter revealed to PEOPLE that she's ready for the world to see her in a different – and surprising way: "I'm a lesbian mom," she says.

Baxter, 62, first started dating women seven years ago, the thought of being gay "had never crossed my mind," she tells PEOPLE. Having been in three failed marriages to men (most famously to actor David Birney), she says of her many difficult years before coming out, "I was never comfortable with myself," but adds, "That doesn't mean I was questioning."

Now in a four-year relationship with building contractor Nancy Locke – the couple have lived together for two years – the actress, who continues to act and run a skincare company says, "I feel like I'm being honest for the first time."

Baxter was open about her newfound identity almost immediately with her five kids. Her son Peter's reaction, like that of his siblings, was both reassuring and supportive. "I just couldn't stop smiling," says Peter, 25 "because she finally figured it out."

Portia de Rossi

Excerpts from Oprah Winfrey Shown
November 2010

"Having to hide something like that just ruined me. It really, really killed me. I had always really loved men - and still do - and just kind of assumed that I would be straight. I think everybody assumes that you're going to be heterosexual. And the thing that made me think that I wasn't was I developed very strong feelings for my best friends. I had a series of mini-heartbreaks throughout my teens because my fantasy of what life could be like with my best friend wasn't shared with my best friend. My best friend wanted to get married to a man and have kids and I just wanted to be with them and that's when I thought something was definitely different about me. But really it took me until I was about 18 when I realized I had to date other lesbians if I was ever going to fulfill that fantasy. Hiding your sexuality is the most horrible way to live and it really does a huge disservice to society, because if everybody who was gay came out in every profession, teachers, doctors, if everybody came out and said 'I'm gay. Who cares?' it would make a big impact to what's happening with all this teenage suicide."

Sophie Ward

Excerpts from: After Ellen *by Locksley Hall,*

August 22, 2006

In 1994, Ward starred in a TV adaptation of

Joanna Trollope's novel *A Village Affair,* about a

married woman with children who falls in love

with another woman. And in December 1996 —

at a time when Ellen DeGeneres was still in the

closet — Ward caused a tabloid uproar in Britain by coming out as a lesbian herself.

When asked about her gradual path toward understanding her sexuality, Ward said: "I don't know how much hormones blind you to certain things. Because I did have a lot of people who said to me afterwards that it wasn't until after they'd had children and that great desire to have children had subsided somewhat, that they felt that they were able to really be themselves."

Ward notes that although she did not identify as a lesbian when she was a teenager, she did have crushes on women. "I knew that I had feelings for women, and I thought possibly I was bisexual," she says. "But I was with my husband when I was so young — almost as soon as I'd left school, I was living with my husband — and I was 19, and I was a stepmum so, I was just sort of getting on with doing that. So it wasn't like I was closeted, or confused, or anything like that at that time. I just felt ... I knew I had feelings for women, but it wasn't a problem, it didn't feel terrible. And it didn't feel like I was locking off part of my personality. Of course in retrospect, I can see that perhaps I was." She denies that coming out publicly at such an early stage in her career, when there were virtually no other well-known actresses to keep her company, was brave. "Of course in an ideal world it would be lovely if there were loads of other role models and people that made you feel, oh, well you're not on your own," Ward says. "But of course you're not on your own, there are loads of gay women".

Ward acknowledges that the fact that there were few openly gay actresses at the time did make her coming-out a bigger deal than it might have been if more actresses had been out. "But on a personal level," she says, "the thing that's hardest is coming out [to the people close to you], the same as anybody else, I think."

Having made the decision to be open with her family, however, the idea of staying closeted publicly just didn't seem like an option to Ward. "That decision not to come out is such a big decision; in a way it's much bigger than coming out," she says. "Because your life has to be so organized."

"Making the decision to not talk about your personal life has many implications for a public figure. It means you can't be seen publicly with your girlfriend," she said. "That you can't ever talk about your girlfriend or partner, that you can't have any kind of social or professional life

173

together where you might be seen." She adds with a laugh, "I think that sounds awfully tiring."

Ward says that she just couldn't envision an alternative to coming out. "It would have been such hard work. Maybe it makes a difference having a family, I don't know, but ... how would [staying closeted publicly] have worked in my family, with my children? Would I not have come out to them?" She laughs at the thought. "Would I have separate households somehow, or would I have to tell them not to tell anyone? It's just impossible to think about. So it wasn't particularly a brave decision; it was just a decision that was going to make life better for everybody. So ... that was that."

48 More

Famous

Lesbians

Amanda Moore

Model

Jodie Foster

Actress

Alexandra Hedison
Actress

Lea Delaria
Actress, Comedian

Amber Heard

Actress, model

Lily Tomlin
Comedian

Cynthia Nixon

Actress

Leisha Hailey

Actress, Musician

Drew Barrymore
(bisexual) Actress

Rosie O'Donnell
Comedian, Talk Show
Host

Guinevere Turner

Actress, Writer, Director

Samantha Fox

Musician

Heather Matarazzo
Actress

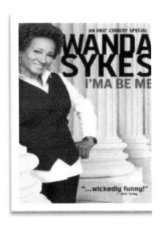

Wanda Sykes
Actress, Comedian,
Writer

Heather Peace

Actress

Brandi Carlile

Musician

Jane Lynch

Actress, Comedian

Clementine Ford

Actress

Jill Bennett and Cathy DeBuono
Actresses

Cat Cora
Iron Chef

Amanda Bearse
Actress

Ann Bancroft
Author, Teacher,
Adventurer

Alison Bechdel
Artist-Comics

Cherry Jones
Actress

Ilene Chaiken
Producer

Kate Clinton
Political Humorist,
Author

Phyllida Lloyd
Theatre Director

Rita Mae Brown
Author

Ruby Rose
Model

Sandra Bernhard
Comedian

Sarah Gilbert
Actress

Sarah Paulson
Actress

Kate Brown
(bisexual) Politician

Sarah Waters
Author

Katherine Brooks
Actress

Sheryl Swoopes
(bisexual) WNBA
player

Lisa Cholodenko
Director, Writer

Suze Orman
Financial Advisor,
Motivational Speaker

Mary Gauthier
Musician

Tegan and Sara
Musicians

Michelle Bonilla
Actress

Val McDermid
Author

Margaret Cho
Author, Comedian

Vicki Randle
Musician

Melissa Etheridge
Musician

Nancy Ruth
Ontario Senator

17551033R10102

Printed in Great Britain
by Amazon